Choke Holds Scandal

Role-Play Peacegame™

Role-Play Peacegame™

Robert Scanlon and David W. Felder

Wellington Press

Choke Holds Scandal

Role-Play Peacegame™

Robert Scanlon and David W. Felder

Wellington Press
9601-30 Miccosukee Road
Tallahassee, FL 32309
www.peacegames.com
Peacegames@aol.com

Library of Congress Control Number: 2010920794
Cataloging in Publication Data
Robert Scanlon
Choke Holds Scandal / Role-Play Peacegames
p. cm.
ISBN 978-1-57501-007-6
1. Peace 2. Conflict Resolution 3. Title
303.6/9 Sca or 363.2 Sca

Contents

Introduction 5

Directions 7

Lesson in Conflict Resolution 8

The Facts 28

NAACP 32

Police Department 34

District Attorney 36

What Actually Happened 38

Games in Instruction

Rating of Games for Reading Level 40

Suggestions for Getting Started 40

The Use of Games in Instruction 41

Use of Games for Workshops 42

List of Role-Play Peacegames™ Games 43

Boardgames 51

About the Authors 53

Introduction

Role-Play Peacegames™ are designed as an introduction to the role of mediation in resolving disputes. Wellington Press hopes that those using these games will decide to learn more about mediation. There is much to learn.

The term "participant" refers to the people who have a dispute, and the term "mediator" refers to a person who helps the participants reach a settlement.

In each game there is a fact sheet that explains the background of the dispute. The mediator reads this at the start of each game. Do not alter or add facts.

The parties to the conflict each have pages that cannot be read by anyone else. These pages list what each participant wants.

Role-Play Peacegames™ from Wellington Press assign percentage values to each item to indicate which items are most important. Participants can use the percentage scores to see how their interests are served in the final settlement. The mediator's score is the average of the scores of the participants. All players have an interest in reaching an agreement because if no agreement is reached, then everyone has a score of zero. The game can also be played without scoring.

Participants are expected to realistically perform the roles they are given, and to make an honest effort to reach a settlement. Since this is a game that develops the skills of mediation, the participants should not try to arrive at a settlement through their own negotiation skills, but should depend on the skills of the mediator.

Directions

If you are not familiar with Conflict Resolution principles then read and do the exercises in the Lesson in Conflict Resolution.

When you are ready, play the game.

Decide who will be the mediator and who will be each participant in the conflict.

The mediator and the participants should not look at pages other than their own.

1. Someone reads the "Introductory Statement" aloud.
2. Someone reads the fact page aloud.
3. Everyone studies their pages. Participants in the conflict study their parts. The mediator studies the page on mediation.
4. The mediator begins the session.
5. The participants can meet together and also can request to meet separately with the mediator.
6. Try to write down an agreement
7. Compare your agreement to What Actually Happened where applicable. Don't look at **What Actually Happened** until you are finished and don't look at pages other than your own.

Lesson in Conflict Resolution

Introduction

People have always been interested in learning ways of resolving conflicts. Even those people who want to go to war with others prefer to have those on their side settle their conflicts without violence. It is only recently, however, that the study of conflict resolution has begun in earnest. In this chapter some of the vocabulary, concepts and applications of the new discipline of conflict resolution are presented.

Responses to Conflict

There are various responses that can be taken to the existence of conflict. Several of these are presented.

CONCEPTS: Conflict Avoidance, Negotiation, Arbitration, and Mediation

Conflict Avoidance occurs when a party to a conflict decides to forgo his or her interest in favor of another party. Conflict avoidance is also called capitulation. People choose this strategy when they decide that trying to pursue their interest is not worth the trouble.

Negotiation occurs when disputants try to reach an agreement that will satisfy the basic self-interest of each party. Negotiation depends on the ability to make promises that can be kept.

Arbitration occurs when parties to a dispute either decide to or are forced to accept the decision of a third party. The third party is called an arbitrator or arbiter.

Mediation occurs when disputants decide their own process and decision settlement. A mediator helps the parties develop options and see options realistically so that they can come to an agreement that all parties accept. Mediation is a voluntary process.

Mediation

We will examine mediation because that is the peacemaking role that individuals can hope to play. A mediator helps to bring disputants together. Certain skills aid the mediator in this process. One skill is to have the disputants focus on interests.

Conflict of Interest

A conflict of interest occurs when two or more parties want something — the attainment of which by one precludes the attainment by the other. Conflicts are real or perceived states of competing interests. People may perceive that they have a conflict when do not actually have competing interests.

Interests versus Positions

Interests are end results such as the satisfaction of needs.

Positions are views people hold regarding the means they might use to achieve ends.

The difference between interests and positions is the same as between ends and means. It is best to focus on interests and not positions because there may be more than one means to an end.

Person Centered, Position Centered, Interest Centered

Person centered disputes exist because of the personalities involved.

Position centered disputes exist because people are taking incompatible positions. Another name for position centered disputes is "issue centered." Positions are statements regarding means for the achievement of ends.

Interest centered disputes exist because people have conflicting interests. If one person gets what he or she wants then the other parties cannot get all of what they want. The emphasis is on end results and the satisfaction of needs.

Exercise 1: Name ________________

Directions: Indicate what is true of each example using these choices:
A) This is centered on personalities.
B) This is centered on positions.
C) This is centered on interests.

1. The union would like to discuss health benefits and wage increases.
2. We must stick together as a people if we want to make progress.
3. Neither the United States nor the Russia would benefit from the spread of nuclear weapons to more countries.
4. Let us begin the mediation session by examining the statements made by each party in the dispute.
5. We will begin this mediation session with each person stating what they think of the other person.
6. I would like to begin this mediation session by asking each person to say what bothers them about the existing situation.
7. I don't see how Kate can talk to that guy.
8. You saw our list of demands. That is all we are here to discuss.
9. Mark does not see how Joe can put up with Sue's flirting with others.

10. Neither the Jones nor the Smiths will benefit from the fighting. .
11. My fellow brothers in the fraternity and I will stand firm on our decision.
12. I will never pass this class as long as Dr. Brooks is the instructor.
13. We will begin this mediation session with each person stating what they think the decision should be.
14. Our viewpoint is clearly stated in our sheet outlining what we think the final settlement should contain.
15. Let me tell you how I am hurt by what has happened.

Outcomes

It is best to get the parties to a dispute to discuss their interests, rather than personalities or positions, because there are techniques for reconciling interests.

Competition, Compromise, Collaboration & Cooperation

Competition is a strategy that a person in conflict may follow which would, if successful, result in the person getting all of what they want, with the other parties to the conflict getting nothing.

Compromise is a strategy that aims at give and take so the result is 50-50.

Collaboration is a strategy that involves the integration of interests so that a disputant helps the party they have disputes with get what they want while still protecting their own interest.

Cooperation is working together for mutual gain and sharing the gain equally.

Chart Showing Interests

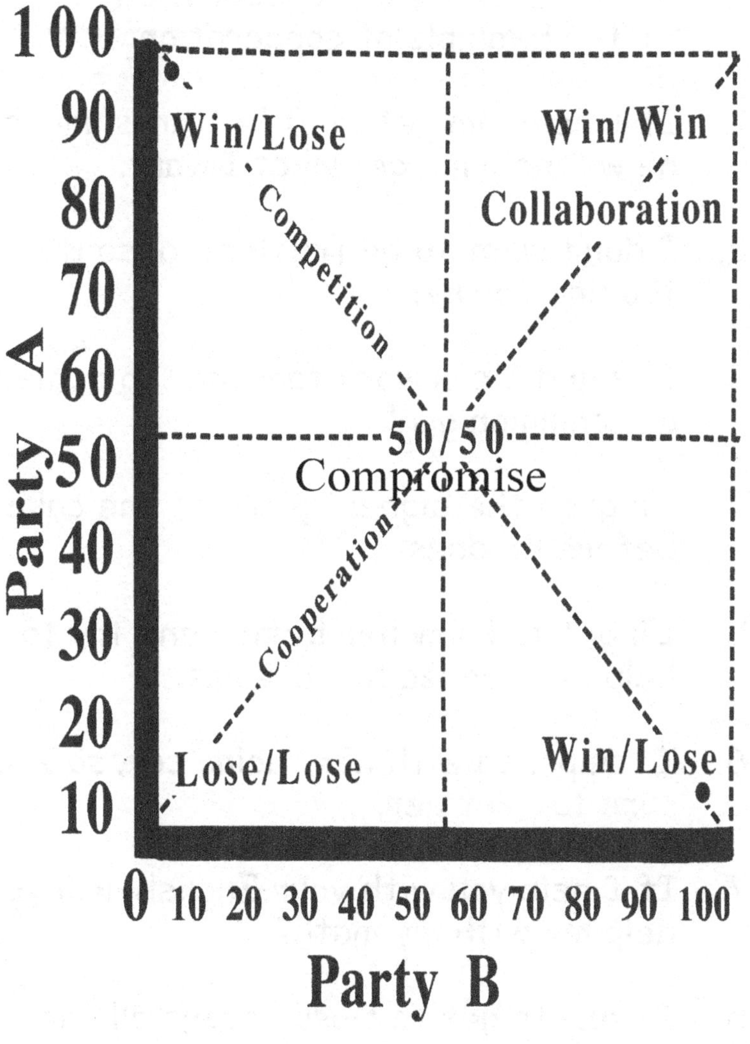

Exercise 2: Name ____________________

A) Example of competition
B) Example of compromise
C) Example of collaboration
D) Example of cooperation

1. If I help him get what he wants, maybe he will help me get what I want.

2. I don't want to be frustrated, so it's too bad for her.

3. She and I can work together to achieve our common goal.

4. I'll grab the biggest piece of the cake before he does.

5. I'll get to know her better and try to help her realize her dreams.

6. I tampered with her racing car, so I am sure to beat her.

7. If I help you with your English, will you help me with my math?

8. I want to get to class before all the seats are taken.

9. Since I don't want her to get a better grade than I get, I won't let her know the assignment.

10. He and I can study together so we can both pass the course.

11. I watched my show for thirty minutes and he watched the basketball game for thirty minutes.

12. We want a twenty percent salary increase and don't care what it does to the company.

13. We will meet you half way on our demands for a twenty percent salary increase.

14. We would be willing to take a salary increase in the form of a stock-sharing program if this would help the company.

15. You heard my offer. Take it or leave it.

Asking Questions

The mediator's job of helping the disputants come to agreement is best aided when all sides are aiming at a solution where everyone wins. The ideal is to have collaboration, but compromise may be the best solution possible. The main tool that the mediator has is the ability to ask the parties to the conflict questions that will help them be realistic about what the other side might agree to. The next section discusses the different types of questions a mediator might ask.

CONCEPT: Open Questions vs. Closed Questions

Procedure:
Ask yourself, "Is the answer yes or no?" If so, it is a closed question. If the range of answers is open then it is an open question.

Examples:
"What do you hope to get from this process?" (open)
"Are you here to try to reach an agreement?" (closed)

CONCEPT: Direct vs. Indirect

Procedure:
Ask, "Do they have to answer?" If yes, it is a direct question. If no, it is an indirect question.

Example:
"What do you propose?" (direct)
"I wonder why she is resisting your offer?" (indirect)

Note: It is possible to combine the distinction between open and closed with the distinction between direct and indirect. The four possibilities, and examples of each, are:

Open Direct
Why do you think he will do it?
Open Indirect
I wonder what he will do?
Closed Direct
Do you think he will accept?
Closed Indirect
I wonder if he will accept that?

Exercise 3: Name ____________________

Directions: Indicate what is true of each example using these choices:

A) Open Direct
B) Open Indirect
C) Closed Direct
D) Closed Indirect

1. I wonder why she hasn't suggested a settlement along these lines?

2. Do you think that your proposal will be accepted?

3. Would you be willing to state this directly to her?

4. What do you think his response will be to your proposal?

5. I wonder if she will accept your offer?

6. I wonder why Bob chose to go with Plan B?

7. Why do you think that Bob decided to go with Plan B?

8. I wonder what he will do at the next meeting?

9. Will you talk to him?

10. Do you feel that they will do as you suggest?

11. Do you think she will accept your offer?

12. I wonder if you would be willing to say that to her directly?

13. Do you think he will mind?

14. What do you think is her reason for being there?

15. I wonder what she might think?

Mediation Procedure
Short Version

1. INTRODUCE YOURSELF.

Ask the disputants their names. Explain that your job is to help them reach an agreement and that the process is voluntary. Thank them for coming.

2. ASK FOR THE JOB.

Have the parties commit themselves to the process by asking "Would you like me to be your mediator?"

3. LIST GROUND RULES.

Everybody agrees to try to solve the problem. No name calling or insults are allowed.

4. ASK ONE PARTY TO STATE HIS OR HER GENERAL VIEWPOINT.

Participants take turns speaking.

Mediator Role in Detail

I. At the beginning of the Session

1. INTRODUCE YOURSELF. Explain that your job as a mediator is to help the parties in the dispute reach an agreement and that the process is voluntary. Thank them for coming.
2. ASK FOR THE JOB. Get the parties to commit themselves to the process by asking "Would you like me to be your mediator?"
3. LIST GROUND RULES.
   The rules are that everyone agrees to try to solve the problem, there will be no name-calling, or insults, and everyone gets to speak without interruption.
4. ASK EACH OF THE DISPUTANTS IF THEY AGREE TO THE RULES.
5. EXPLAIN THAT EVERYTHING SAID IN A MEDIATION IS CONFIDENTIAL (Except when there are health dangers).
6. EXPLAIN THAT PARTIES IN THE DISPUTE MAY REQUEST TO SPEAK TO THE MEDIATOR PRIVATELY. The Mediator may also request to speak to participants privately. Anything said in private can be kept private.

II. Let Each Person Tell His or Her Side of the Conflict

1. CHOOSE THE ORDER OF THE SPEAKERS.
2. ASK ONE PARTY TO STATE HIS OR HER VIEWPOINT.
3. REPEAT WHAT YOU HAVE HEARD, TO SHOW THAT YOU UNDERSTOOD WHAT THEY SAID. Restate the facts they presented or make a statement about the feelings they expressed to show that you have understood what they said.
   Repeat Facts by stating "Let me see if I understand.. You are saying . . . "
   Restate Views by saying "So it seems to you that. . ."
   Describe their feelings by saying "It sounds like your feeling is . . . "
4. LET EACH PERSON SPEAK, AND SHOW THAT YOU ARE LISTENING.

III. Try to Understand the Problems

1. HELP PEOPLE UNDERSTAND EACH OTHER AND THE PROBLEMS BY ASKING QUESTIONS SUCH AS:
   "Could you tell us more about that"
   "How did you feel about that?"
   "What would you like to see happen?"
2. CHECK TO MAKE SURE YOU UNDERSTOOD EACH PERSON, AND HELP THEM TO UNDERSTAND EACH OTHER.
   "I heard you say. . ." "Is that right?"
   "Do you understand why the other party feels as they do?"

IV. Help Participants Find a Solution

1. ASK EACH PERSON:
   "What can you do to help solve this?"
   "Can you think of other alternatives?"
2. ENCOURAGE THE PARTICIPANTS TO COME TO AN AGREEMENT. Ask participants while they are together, or while they are meeting separately with you:
   "What would you be willing to accept?"
   "What do you suppose the other party (or parties) will accept?"
3. TRY TO WRITE DOWN AN AGREEMENT.
4. IF AGREEMENT IS REACHED, CONGRATULATE THE PARTICIPANTS FOR REACHING AN AGREEMENT.

Choke Holds Scandal

Role-Play Peacegame™

PARTIES

NAACP

Police Department

District Attorney

Choke Holds Scandal

The Facts

On July 12, 1983, police arrested a 22-year-old African American named Spencer Allard on charges of disorderly conduct. While being transported to the Eastside Memorial Hospital Psychiatric Department (Allard has a history of treatment for psychosis), he kicked out the windows of the police car he was riding in. When the two officers stopped the car to subdue him, they applied a choke hold to the enraged and psychotic Allard, who went into cardiac arrest and died. The Sanford Clarion newspaper revealed the next day in their coverage of the incident that Allard was the ninth young African-American male to die in police custody since 1980–all from the application of choke holds during attempts to subdue them. No white suspect had ever died after having been placed in a choke hold.

The Rev. James Potter of the Folcroft AME Church organized a press conference the next day of African-American community leaders and businessmen to denounce the use of choke holds, demand an end to their use and call for the prosecution of the two officers who applied the choke hold to Allard. State Rep. Joe Garry, who was rumored to be planning to run against Mayor Bradshaw in the 1994 Mayoral election, used the occasion to personally attack Mayor Bradshaw. District Attorney Terry Robbins responded by telling an audience of police officers that he had "no plans" to take the Allard death before the Grand Jury, and that he personally considered choke holds a legitimate means of subduing suspects who "could not be reasoned with because of their mental condition." The Sanford Clarion reported the next day that many African-Americans interpreted this as a racial slur. District Attorney Robbins claimed the next day that he was referring to persons with mental illness.

In this racially charged climate there were a number of incidents of harassment between the police and African Americans. The governor of the state, Governor Mills, decided to appoint a special prosecutor to review the choke holds deaths, and to consider taking the case away from District Attorney Robbins' jurisdiction.

The city's business community began to grumble that, once again, racial incidents were giving the city a bad name.

Reverend Potter and his coalition kept up a steady pressure, taking affidavits from dozens of young African-American males who had been subdued by choke holds. The Sanford Municipal Police Department (SMPD) began to threaten a strike.

Now Mayor Bradshaw has formed a task force representing all the affected parties–the NAACP, the Police Department, and District Attorney Robbins and asked them to review the SMPD policy on choke holds and other means of subduing suspects. He has promised to implement their recommendation, but only if it is unanimous.

Choke Holds Scandal

Your General Viewpoint

Since we began to investigate this matter, we have uncovered conclusive proof that choke holds are routinely used against African-American suspects, but rarely against others. We have the testimony on file of hundreds of our young men injured by choke holds, and dozens of them who have been tortured by stun guns as well. We were not aware of the stun gun problem until we began interviewing the victims of choke holds. Many of our people have been subjected to both forms of brutality. We will not tolerate cover-ups that set white murderers in uniform free while our young men die in shame and degradation.

NAACP

What You Want

1. The use of choke holds on non-deranged suspects must stop! 30%

2. The use of choke holds on deranged suspects must stop! 30%

3. The police must stop carrying stun guns. 20%

4. The investigation of the choke hold deaths must continue. 20%

Choke Holds Scandal

Your General Viewpoint

Once again, civilians who seem to love criminals are trying to tie our hands while they roam free-and are free to kill us any-time they can get our guns away from us! End this persecution of honest cops who are just doing their duty. Are we going to have a special task force investigating us every time the media needs headlines?

Police Department

What You Want

1. Disband the special prosecutor. 20%

2. Uphold the department policy allowing choke holds at the discretion of the officer. 20%

3. Uphold the department policy permitting choke holds in the case of deranged suspects. 20%

4. Uphold the department policy allowing officers to carry stun guns. 20%

5. Set up a commission to investigate why so-called black leaders are always so supportive of black criminals. 20%

Choke Holds Scandal

Your General Viewpoint

I have always supported a strong police department, and I have consistently campaigned against elements in our community who care more for the criminals among us than they do for the needs of decent people. The existing SMPD policy on subduing violent suspects seems good to me–let's just try to make it a little better.

District Attorney Robbins

What You Want

1. Transfer the investigation of the choke hold deaths back to my office. 25%

2. Eliminate the use of choke holds in the handling of suspects who are not deranged. 25%

3. Let the officers keep their stun guns. 25%

4. Let the officers continue to use stun guns on suspects who appear deranged. 25%

Choke Holds Scandal

What Actually Happened

The task force debated for ten months, while the members spent more time grandstanding for their constituencies than they did trying to write a new policy. Consequently, Mayor Bradshaw disbanded the task force and began to work on a policy with the assistance of a paid consultant in police policy from out-of- state. In the middle of this task, the special prosecutor appointed by Governor Mills concluded her investigation by bringing involuntary manslaughter charges against the officers involved in two of the choke hold deaths, but not the officers involved in the death of Spencer Allard. The officers who were charged all pleaded guilty under an agreement whereby they were fined and placed on probation, but spared a jail term. The final report of the Grand Jury that heard the case under the special prosecutor's guidance recommended in their final report that choke holds and stun guns be banned and Mayor Bradshaw ordered that this be done. The Mayor was relieved that the burden of the decision had been taken away from him.

Rating of Games for Reading Level

All Role-Play Peacegames™ have been rated as suitable for grade seven though college. Alan Markwood of the National Institute for Dispute Resolution included a rating of the reading level in an article on the games that appeared in their journal on Conflict Resolution, *The Fourth R*. These games have been used successfully to teach conflict resolution skills, history, and have found many other uses, including being used to teach English in Eastern Europe.

Suggestions for Getting Started

In using the games with a group of eight to a hundred people it is desirable to show a list of games that are available and then have individuals volunteer to take particular games, and then have others join them according to how many players are needed for each game.

The Use of Games in Instruction

It is best to start with the instruction on conflict resolution and spend an hour on that before doing the games. The lesson on conflict resolution could take one or two hours of classroom time, with the option of giving the exercises as an assignment if done in two sessions. Doing the games can be done in an hour.

It is up the instructor to decide how much time to spend on conflict resolution skills versus learning about particular conflicts. A history class might want to get into the games with a minimum amount of time on conflict resolution while a class on conflict resolution might want to spend a longer time on the Lesson in Conflict Resolution.

In general students feel more comfortable starting with personal conflicts, such as are found in the Teenage Conflicts and Family Conflicts series, before tackling world conflicts. It may be desirable to have students do Role-Play Peacegames™ on both types of conflicts.

The Use of Games in Workshops

These games can be used as the basis for workshops for in house education credits or for presentations at conferences. All one has to do for an exciting workshop session is present a short lesson in conflict and then have participants do a game. Successful workshops have been done by the author at the Safe Schools conferences in New Orleans and Boston, Chautaugua Assemblies, before religious groups, and before history and international affairs organizations.

Any game that is relevant to your organization might be used for a workshop. People of all ages enjoy role-play games. A good plan for a workshop might be to make introductory remarks and perhaps use the Lesson in Conflict Resolution and then jump into doing the games. Successful workshops have been conducted for periods of from one hour to three hours. A full day of activities could be planned around doing several different games. Feel free to be creative. You do not need permission to use these games as the basis for a workshop.

Books for History

All books listed can be ordered by ISBN numbers wherever books are sold. To get the ISBN number, add the numbers in parenthesis next to each title to the end of 978-1-57501.

American History (000-7)

American Revolution (001-4)
U. S. Constitutional Convention (228-5)
Civil War (009-0)
Reconstruction (112-7)
U.S. in Vietnam (229-2)
Election 2000 (199-8)
Race Relations Summit (118-9)

World History (221-6)

Thirty Years War (231-5)
Seven Years War (151-6)
Napoleonic Wars (119-6)
First World War (027-4)
Vietnam War (226-1)
Iraq Invades Kuwait (035-9)
United Nations Reform (111-0)

World Conflicts (222-3)

Test Ban Treaty (233-9)
Seabed Arms Control (128-8)
Vietnam War (226-1)
Camp David (006-9)
Star Wars Controversies (129-5)
Iraq Invades Kuwait (035-9)
Obama's Mideast Diplomacy (117-2)

Balkans Conflict (002-1)

Bosnia & Herzegovina (004-5)
Macedonia Conflict (042-7)
First World War (027-4)
Ethnic Cleansing (021-2)
Kosovo Conflict (039-7)

Middle East Conflicts (044-1)

Camp David (006-9)
Oslo (371-8)
Israel and Syria (235-3)
Israel and Lebanon (040-3)
Middle East Regional Issues (045-8)
Obama's Mideast Diplomacy (117-2)
Iraqi Political Parties (036-6)
Iraq and It's Neighbors (370-1)

Iraq Conflict (365-7)

Iraq Invades Kuwait (035-9)
Kurdish Issues (366-4)
Iraqi Political Parties (036-6)
Iraq and It's Neighbors (370-1)

Social Studies, Civics

Courtroom Conflicts (013-7)

Criminal Court (014-4)
Small Claims Court (147-9)
Civil Court (008-3)
Divorce Court (018-2)
Family Court (024-3)
Juvenile Court (037-3)

Police & Community (115-8)

Curfew (015-1)
Civilian Review Board (010-6)
Removing the Homeless (133-2)
Choke Holds Scandal (007-6)
Race Riot after a Verdict (114-1)
Racial Tension in High School (113-4)
Gang Fighting (029-8)

Environmental Conflicts (019-9)

Selenium Contamination (153-0)
Everglades Revival (132-5)
River Cleanup (131-8)
Development Issues (146-2)
Conservation & Indian Rights (012-0)
Test Ban Treaty (233-9)
Star Wars Controversies (129-5)

Life & Counseling

Marital Conflicts (043-4)

Marriage Decision (368-8)
Unmarried and Pregnant (228-8)
Relocation Conflict (134-9)
Raising Biracial Children (135-6)
Deciding Where to Retire (016-8)
Money Problems (046-5)
Same Sex Equal Partners (130-1)

Divorce Conflicts (017-5)

Untangling the Finances (369-5)
Money Problems (046-5)
They Work at the Same Place (232-2)
She Wants Her Share (149-3)
Affair with Lover's Daughter (223-0)
Mixed Faiths (372-5)
Divorce Court (018-2)

Rehabilitation Conflicts (199-8)

Rehabilitation Center (136-3)
Training Center (032-8)
Extended Care Center (022-9)
Rehabilitation Hospital (367-1)
Spinal Center (145-5)

Elementary School, Guidance

Teenage Conflicts (234-6)

Gang Fighting (029-8)
Love Triangle (041-0)
Blended Family Conflicts (003-8)
Sexual Harassment (150-8)
Breaking Up (005-2)
Juvenile Court (037-3)
Unmarried and Pregnant (227-8)

Family Conflicts (023-6)

Grades in School (030-4)
Visiting Divorced Dad (225-4)
Helping with Baby-sitting (031-1)
Single Mom's Boyfriend (148-6)
Raising Biracial Children (135-6)
Juvenile Court (037-3)
Family Court (024-3)

Multicultural & Racial (047-2)

Race Relations Summit (118-9)
Hiring More Black Teachers (033-5)
Raising Biracial Children (135-6)
Racial Tension in High School (113-4)
Multicultural Curriculum (048-9)
Farrakhan Visits Campus (026-7)
Race Riot after a Verdict (114-1)

Boardgames

WIN/WIN: The Peace Game (364-0)

Kingdom of Ends: Kant's Ethics (363-3)

Utilitarian Game: Mill's Ethics (362-6)

WIN/WIN:
The Peace Game

WIN/WIN is an enjoyable board game and also a serious research tool. Based on the Prisoner's Dilemma model used by many peace researchers, WIN/WIN can be used to examine how alternative approaches to conflict increase or decrease cooperation.

WIN/WIN forces players to choose between being aggressive and being cooperative. When any player lands on special squares they must choose whether to buy a bomb or not buy a bomb, to pollute or not polute, to contribute to the commons or be a freeloader, and whether to bully others or live in peace. Each player has cards with these choices and must make decisions without knowing whether the other players are choosing to be cooperative or aggressive. Players cover the card that indicates their decision and then everyone shows their choice at the same time.

Each game has instructions, pages on the logic of the choices, suggestions of topics that can be researched such as "How can cooperation be increased?, and pages on the results of past research.

KINGDOM OF ENDS GAME:
Kant's Ethics in a Board Game

Immanuel Kant, a devout Christian, wanted an ethics based on reason that would parallel Christian Ethics. Kant tried to envision human beings relating at the highest level, with people treating each other as ends and not as means. The goal of ethics is to be a person who is fit to interact with others at the highest moral level, the Kingdom of Ends.

In this board game players go from one neighborhood to another, starting in a high crime neighborhood where people obey the law only from fear, and players must show that they are virtuous enough to progress to a low crime neighborhood where people act from a combination of fear and duty to progress to the Kingdom of Ends where people act from a sense of duty.

This is an enjoyable game that makes Kant's ethical philosophy come alive as players learn the distinction between acting in accord with duty and acting from a sense of duty. It has practical implications as players learn that virtue is its own reward.

UTILITARIAN GAME: Ethics of Bentham and Mill

As the Utilitarian game begins there are no laws, and players can rob each other without any deterrent. Players then vote on laws, using Mill's Ethics in a Board Game to figure out the punishments. Each player is a different type of Utilitarians and on the "Quiz" space must answer questions according to the type of Utilitarian that they are: Ideal versus Limited, Hedonist versus Epicurean, and Act versus Rule Utilitarian. Players have fun as they learn about the Utilitarian philosophy that aims at providing the greatest good for the greatest number. This is an important philosophy because in a democracy with majority rule, and people voting for what will benefit themselves, we are prone to achieving the greatest good for the greatest number.

The game is set up so that players discover the advantages and disadvantages of this ethical system. As with all morality games it forces players to apply principles in making their decisions.

Authors

Dr. David W. Felder is a former Professor in Philosophy at Florida A & M University and Professor in Peace Studies at Florida State University. Dr. Felder has made numerous presentations at national and international conferences in both fields, from Montreal to Jerusalem to Moscow. His publications include *Reasoning Skills for Handling Conflict, Key to High Scores on Standardized Tests,* and *Role-Play Peacegames™* that he sometimes writes with others. He can be contacted at Peacegames@aol.com.

Captain Robert Scanlon retired from the Washington D. C. Municipal Police Department. He worked in many areas of police work including developing evaluation tools.

Made in the USA
Monee, IL
04 November 2026

67380394R00036